EXPRESSIONS INSPIRED VOLUME ONE

Rhymes, Reality, and Spoken Word

By Labretta Goines Donegan

EXPRESSIONS INSPIRED
VOLUME ONE

Rhymes, Reality, and Spoken Word

Preface

This eclectic collection of poetry was inspired by our life events, emotions and experiences, and anything else that simply moves us to express how we may truly feel when it comes to our personal struggles, love and relationships, our spirituality, self-worth, and being imperfect people living in an imperfect world. Traditional rhymes and free verse come together to take you on familiar paths of both light and darkness. That familiar path of light could be encouraging words to keep pushing forward regardless of our situation and circumstances, or it could simply be the excitement of meeting a new love. That familiar path of darkness could be the pain and hurt that's felt from depression, betrayal or injustice. Smile, laugh, reflect and wonder, and maybe even cry a little when reading Expressions Inspired, and be reminded of the fact that you are only human.

To my sons, Timothy, Jr. and Christopher Blake Donegan:

A sense of humor that keeps me laughing for days
You each have a unique personality of your own
You can sometimes have hard-headed ways
But without you, my house would not be a home

Our bond is an unbroken circle
Love,

Mama

Table of Contents

My Rights 8

What I Got 9

Words 11

"I" 12

Go Deep 13

We Do Need You 14

Who We Be 15

The Truth 16

You Don't Cry No More 17

Sisters 18

The New Me Realization 19

Who Do You Think You Are? 20

Falling 21

Speechless 21

That Kiss 22

You Can't Hide 22

Learn Who I Am 23

Soulful Respect 24

It's Not You 26

Who Can Stand? 27

The System 28

Wide Open 29

Tranquility 30

Initiative 30

Chocolate Child 31

Love Hopeless 32

Under The Scope 33

Misunderstood 34

Colors 35

You & I 36

Set Yourself Free 38

What He Loves   39

An Interesting Question   40

Missing You   42

The Hole   43

Melee In My Mind   44

Feel Sorry For Him   45

Time & Unforseen Occurrence   46

Unworthy   47

What I Feel   48

Spoil Me   49

He Said   50

Our Life is Music   51

Wish I Knew   52

The One Thing I Can't Stand   53

Cold   54

Played   55

Sister Girl & Brother Man   56

Mind vs. Heart   57

Obey   58

Soul Food   59

A Family Strong   60

My Feel Good Feeling   60

Childhood   61

In Denial (I Think He Loves Me)   62

Negativity   63

Take Me Away   64

The Wicked One   65

Random Thoughts   66

My #1 Fan   68

Acknowledgements   69

The Inspiration   70

MY RIGHTS

Today, I'm giving up my rights:

The right to be filled with anger and bitterness

The right to hold on to the past

The right to feel sorry for myself

The right to trust no one in the belief that everyone is untrustworthy of me

The right to convince myself that my life will never change for the better

I'm giving up my rights in order to be a slave to peace, love, strength, and faith. No more freedom of a pessimistic spirit.

WHAT I GOT

Do you want what I got?

I got issues.
I got let downs and disappointments.
I got the could've, should've, would'ves.
I got thrown under the bus.
I got punked, lied to, made a fool of, scammed, hustled, hoodwinked, I fell
for the okie-doke ya'll!

I got problems.
I got a hundred dollars worth of groceries, and a fridge that's still bare.
I got money, and I'm still broke.
I got bills.
I got to make a dollar out of 15 cents.
I got to rob Peter in order to pay Paul, so Paul can pay Tyrone for that $50
he let him hold 'til payday.

I got headaches and backaches.
I got stomach aches and heartaches.
I got worries and sleepless nights.
I got sleepless nights wondering will both my sons survive in this unfair,
wicked world.

I got sleepless nights wondering will tonight be my asthmatic son's last
breath of life.
I got sleepless nights wondering if the cancer I had will return.
I got to get a grip ya'll, before I lose my mind.

But what I got, ain't much different than what everybody else got.

I got a roof over my head.
I got clean water to drink and food to eat.
I got clothes on my back and shoes on my feet.
I got abilities and capabilities.
I got perspective ya'll!

I got a strong support system that's got my back.
I got family.
I got friends.
I got love.
I got blessings.
I got prayer and an Almighty God who invites me to draw close to Him so He will draw close to me.
I got life, through God's son, our reigning king, Jesus Christ.
I got life!
My life…
I am thankful for my life.
And I am thankful for what I got.

WORDS

Tangled in a web of lies

Drowning in a pool of deceit

Tortured by the stare of evil eyes

Evil eyes who want to assassinate my character with malicious slander and beat my reputation to a bloody pulp

Their rage is fueled with the ammunition of deep-seated hatred

A lynch mob of hostility that would love nothing more than to watch my dignity perish by the noose that hangs from the tree of despair

A deadly weapon of poisonous tongues speaking words that can completely destroy me and who I am

But I'm still here. And I ain't going nowhere, standing on my mountaintop of endurance.
But the main thing about it is, I'm still standing

My perserverance is power, my existence is vital, and it will never be terminated by words

"I"

I am the one who's most likely to succeed
I can find a way out if possible
I can endure about as much as I can stand
I triumph when I feel unstoppable

I work hard just to get myself through
I rest my soul when I wear myself down
I am not immune to the pressures of the world
I can sometimes fall to pieces on the ground

I am not perfect nor a supernatural wonder
I am just a simple human being
I know my life is still valuable and precious
I am worth more than the ordinary eye is seeing

I am the moon and stars that give light in the dark
I am the warmth that comes from the sun
I am the earth that your feet walk upon
I am simply a woman

GO DEEP

Dive in, go deep inside my thoughts, my mind
Search for what is unknown to others
Stimulate my brain with intellectual conversation
Discuss spiritual things or the future of our brothers

Go deep inside, learn how I think and reason
What makes me tick, what puts my mind in motion
Learn about my childhood, my goals, my fears
See my imagination run deeper than any ocean

Once deep inside, break it down, dissect it
Carefully examine each fragment for common sense
Feel free to remove any clutter
Make room for more intelligence

Once deep inside, get a better understanding
Of just how beautiful the mind can be
Despite some flaws, it holds precious information
Of the makeup and personality of me

WE DO NEED YOU

Independent women of the millennium

Steppin' high and steppin' proud

Moving mountains and putting out fires

And yet the diva in us sparkles

We can do anything, but the fact still remains

We need your guidance, fathers and brothers

Husbands, we need to be loved and feel loved

We complement you, a supportive right hand

Imagine, a world with only queens and no kings

A very dull and boring place, no doubt

God created us from you

So there is no shame in admitting the fact that we do need you

WHO WE BE

We be standing tall as sequoias
We be battling the evil destroyers

We be cool when it's 100 degrees
We be alright as long as you say please

We be done 'cause you took too long
We be the ones to right the wrong

We be the ones out in the crowd
We be the voices singing out loud

We be workin' sun up, sun down
We be cuttin' up and acting a clown

Who we be are just who we are
Everyday people, who be near or far

We be all different colors under the sun
Everyday people, we are one

THE TRUTH

I am the truth

I am the reality and the actuality

I sugar-coat nothing because I tell it like it is

I get right down to the nitty and the gritty

I am the factuality and the substantiality

I am the whole truth, and nothing but the truth

I am the right stuff for a certainty, accurately and precisely right on time

But don't get it twisted, I'm not just an obnoxious brag

My truism is the real deal, the authentic seal of approval

I am what I am, and it is what it is

I am the truth

And you can't handle it

YOU DON'T CRY NO MORE

Cry myself a river
And drown in my tears
As salty as sea water
Wading deep in my fears

Tears rolling down my face
Just like Niagara Falls
I cried an ocean pacific
Until I heard the call

The call of comforting words
From mother and father wisdom
Remind me of who I am
Removing sorrows' symptoms

Encouraged to never give up
A better life for me is in store
They said "You keep your head up"
"And you don't cry no more"

SISTERS

Where would I be without my sisters
The epitome of strength and endurance
Yet as delicate as a beautiful flower
Giving hope, encouragement and assurance

We can laugh and talk about the good times
We can cry and feel each other's pain
We can even fall out with one another
And then win back friendship's gain

Sisters, I pray for you peace and blessings
Working hard at all the things you do
You know you really got it going on
My sisters, I will always love you

THE NEW ME REALIZATION

Since skinny done ran off and left me, I have a new life now, with my curves.

At first, I didn't take too kindly to my curves wanting to be with me, but now, my feelings are different.

It took me a while to get used to the idea because skinny had been with me all my life and hung around for so long.

I just knew skinny would be with me forever, but I was sadly mistaken. I just looked up one day, and poof, skinny was gone!

I still don't understand why skinny left me. We looked so good together. And skinny was so easy going. When skinny was with me, I could wear whatever I wanted, and I could eat whatever I wanted.

You know what, now that I think about it, maybe it was my over-indulgence of the ice cream, the cheesecake, and all that creamy pasta I would devour that made skinny go away. Maybe I was just out of control and skinny thought it would be best to take a bow and let someone else take the stage. And that's when, my curves made an entrance.

Now, my curves isn't as easy going as skinny was when it comes to the clothes I want to wear. My curves will not hesitate to brashly let me know when I don't look good in certain outfits.

And my curves will also constantly remind me to tighten up, so the next one doesn't creep in and steal me away like a thief in the night.

But I don't think my curves will leave me like skinny did. I know my curves love me. I can tell by the way my curves hug me, and I too, love to embrace my curves!

WHO DO YOU THINK YOU ARE?

Who told you to walk in here like that, looking the way you do? (So easy on the eyes!)

Who told you to keep gazing at me until our eyes finally meet and exchange glances? (Those eyes, I think they're amazing!)

Who said you could intrigue me with your smile and radiate a beaming glow all over my face?

Who said it was ok to impress me with that confident cool swagger, and excite me with anticipation as you slowly make your way across the room? Did I say you could come over here mister? (But, oh, here he comes!)

Who told you to speak with a voice as deep as an ocean, and just make me weak in the knees trying to hang on your every word?

Who said it was alright to take me by the hand for a romantic stroll under the moonlight? (I feel like I'm walking on air!)

And who said you could steal a kiss from me while I just melt in your arms?

Are you the man who wants to be "my" man?

Just who do you think you are?!?!

FALLING

I'm falling

But don't try to catch me

Just let me fall

Fall deep into the abyss of something beautiful-your world

SPEECHLESS

Holding me as if you're afraid to let go
How it makes me feel so good inside

So many things I'd like you to know
But when you kiss me, my thoughts run and hide

I'm simply speechless when you love me
So emotional, how lovely

THAT KISS

Sweeter than a chocolate covered caramel drop
As smooth as silk and refreshing like the wind

So electrifying, didn't want it to stop
Felt so good, didn't want it to end

Sent a chill down my spine and made my heart race
Left me with feelings of pure bliss

Relaxed my soul and put a smile on my face
That remarkable, unforgettable kiss

YOU CAN'T HIDE

A twisted mind with no conscience inside
Duckin' and dodgin'
But you just can't hide

Conniving schemes is what you do
Lie and deny
But God sees through you

A master at playing the pity game
Stutterin' and stammerin'
Pointing the blame

A great Oscar performance
But God knows you lied
Try to out run the truth
But you just can't hide

LEARN WHO I AM

My soul is on empty

And my heart is full of hurt and pain

My mind can no longer comprehend

And my voice is gone, because it no longer wants to be heard

My feet move very slowly, because they're hesitant to take the next step

My hands, afraid to reach out and touch, because I might grab hold of something harmful

My eyes have seen too much

And my ears have heard enough

Emotionally drained, lost in sadness

Held hostage by darkness, and can't see the light

My tears are endless

And the thought of any hope seems hopeless

I am depression, but some call me the blues

Get to know me, understand me, pray for me, just don't give up on me, and please don't ignore me

I am depression

Learn who I am, and be a savior of struggling souls

SOULFUL RESPECT

Can't you see?
You're losin' me

You're losin' us
Don't miss the bus

I need you cool
Not acting a fool

A mind that's fresh
No selfishness

Gentle, yet strong
Not a tyrant, that's wrong

Attentive, fulfilling needs
Not choking like weeds

A reliable pair of hands
No laziness, no demands

Stability at it's peak
No room for being weak

To nurture my soul
That is the goal

Take care of spiritual health
Love me, love yourself

Love is the key
Christ said to thee

Christ is the model
The perfect role to follow

This soulful respect
Will gain you respect

Think about it, please
Put your mind at ease

For our love to thrive
For our love to survive

IT'S NOT YOU...

We need to talk.

Lately, it seems that we're growing apart, so I feel it's best that we go our separate ways.

But please, understand, it's not you, it's me.

You know how selfish I am, always begging for your love and attention, and always whining about you never spending any time with me.

Don't forget how I always complain when you make up excuses for being lazy and irresponsible, just laying around all day playing video games.

But please, understand, it's not you, it's me.

I can't seem to keep a cool head each time I catch you in a lie.

And my temper really flies off the charts when you cheat on me with other women, wining and dining them with the money you steal from my purse.

Your emotional intelligence is on a whole different level from mine!

So, I think I deserve something different and new, like dignity and respect.

I'm just not the woman for you!

So please, understand, it's not you, it's me.

WHO CAN STAND?

I have no faith in you
Your word cannot be trusted
Your dark clouds hover above
Pain is what your hands have thrusted

Delivering evil at all cost
Just to feed your hunger of deception
Leading the downfall of all humanity
Misguiding them in the wrong direction

Your path is very broad and spacious
Plenty of room for all wicked sins
Twisted thoughts out rule the conscience
A tangled mess of chaos spins

Does anyone have the backbone?
Does anyone have the courage?
To take a stand against you
So decency and righteousness can flourish?

THE SYSTEM

What a pitiful state
The bitterness the hate
The system that our children must grow up in
They're to grow and learn
But in reality they get burned
The condition of this system is a sin

Adults behaving unruly
Treating others so cruelly
Yet, for our children, they're the prime example
To follow your lead
And your words to heed
But your guidance will cause our young ones to trample

There's no real support
Their potential you abort
The system would rather sit back and watch them fail
Foolishness you exhort
Dishonesty is what you court
And to our children, this is the life you sell

WIDE OPEN

Wide open is the horizon of freedom, as I run to grab this freedom by it's shirt tail

Holding on for my dear life

Reaching out beyond the dark skies and it's black rain that pours down on my face

Reaching for the sun to shed some light on the dark side of the equator

The belief of realities though not beheld is my mountain of faith

Wide open I continue to run, holding on to this freedom

And my soul will be refreshed in it's glory

TRANQUILITY

Feel tranquility in your bubble bath

Hear tranquility when little children laugh

See tranquility in the book of Psalms

Speak tranquility to keep it cool and calm

Tranquility, please, rain down on me

Drown me in peace and serenity

Drown me in happiness, completely soak me

Drown me in your splendor, and set me free

INITIATIVE

Feed the hungry, and they will no longer
starve
Share the wealth, and they will no longer be
poor
Console the weepers and they will no longer
shed tears
Give the key of knowledge, and they'll open
the door

Take the initiative to do unto others
As you would like them to do unto you
Offering a hand of kindness and generosity
A pure heart of goodness and virtue

CHOCOLATE CHILD

Chocolate child
Runnin' wild

In the street
Shufflin' her feet

She thinks she's grown
She's all alone

Hard lessons learned
Chocolate child got burned

Kneeling down and prays
For her crooked ways

She ain't never going back
To that side of the track

Chocolate child gonna fight
To do what's right

That chocolate child
Done stop running wild

Done stop shufflin' her feet
Out in the street

And now she has grown
She can hold her own

LOVE HOPELESS

How can I love someone who doesn't love me?
I don't know, you tell me.

Maybe, if you break it down, I might understand,
but at this point, nothing makes sense.

I know what I feel inside.

I feel the torture of knowing there could never be
a true love experience.

It's wishful thinking, an imagination of love's
romance.

Thoughts of what could be, warms my heart and
fills me with hope.

Once reality sets in, tears fall and turn my warm
heart cold, becoming frozen by hurt feelings,
broken by pain and rejection.

Yet, for some reason, my declaration for this love
stirs inside again, and the cycle of false hope
continues 'til the next episode.

How can I love someone who doesn't love me? I
don't know, you tell me.
Then maybe, I can move on with my life.

UNDER THE SCOPE

You're being watched around the clock
From dusk 'til dawn, in a state of shock

Shocked by the fact that all eyes are on you
Just waiting to see what next you will do

Bombarded with questions about your every move
You have no privacy, you have no groove

You have no space, no room to be free
And you barely even have enough air to breathe

Express your feelings and you'll get criticized
Your thoughts and opinions will only be despised

How can you get loose from such a binding rope
Feeling small and insignificant under the scope

MISUNDERSTOOD

I struggled with carrying the weight of being misunderstood.

No matter what I did or didn't do, the weight got heavier and heavier.

Always defending myself and explaining my actions never made my load any lighter.

Hateful words and sarcastic insults were added on top of the stress, anxiety, hurt , and confusion I was carrying.

It wore me out, so I let it go. I gave up and threw in the towel, do you see it on the floor?

Well, for those who think they know me, you can use that same towel to wipe that crazy look off your faces once you realize that I no longer care.

It's not worth my time, it's not worth the back breaking pain.

My heavenly Father now carries that load, because it was too much for me to bear.

And I thank Him, for lifting such a heavy weight off my shoulders! And I simply shake my head at being misunderstood.

COLORS

I'm made from many shades of colors
Colors that represent me
Colors that show who I am
And also who I strive to be

Shades of pink for softness, femininity
Shades of lavender when calm and mellow
A hint of green for being cool and refreshing
My laughter and happiness represented by yellow

Shades of orange for sudden bursts of energy
Flaming red when there's anger inside
Shades of blue when sadness overwhelms me
And gray for the sorrow I can't hide

Black are my worst fears untold
White is for the peace I pray within
Silver are my dreams and aspirations
A golden heart with love pouring in

These shades of colors are plain and simple
But together, make a beautiful rainbow
These colors can also tell the story
Of a woman you just didn't know

YOU & I

You shove me to the left

I make a slide to the right

You demand that I stand still

I keep dancing in circles

You call it a rebellious, independent spirit

I call it a hope for relief

You call your crooked actions tough love

I call it excrutiating abuse

You continue to intimidate and demean

I continue to press forward in prayer

You keep finding ways to keep blocking me

I keep finding ways to rise above it

You manipulate with your hurtful words

I've learned to turn a deaf ear

You accuse me of being cold and evil

I embrace me for displaying self-respect

You try to smother me so I can't breathe

I keep on gasping for air

You no longer have control over me

And I am free, like feathers blowing in the wind

SET YOURSELF FREE

A prisoner of your own dark thoughts
Afraid of humiliating rejection
Locked up inside your own world
Chained to the fears of oppression

Trapped in a cold, lonely place
Surrounded by only four walls
No windows or doors to be opened
No hope when opportunity calls

Release yourself from this torture
Break out and set yourself free
From the torment of a depressed soul
And how sad it thinks your life should be

WHAT HE LOVES

My mind intrigues him.

He peers into my innermost thoughts, and interacts with my emotional
well-being.

He loves to learn who I am in order to know how to love me.
He loves what's inside my heart.

He loves my humility, and also my ability to display strength and courage.

I stand out from the rest, being different arouses his curiosity.
He doesn't see me as the girl who use to be a size 2, he simply loves the
woman that I am.

My goofy laugh, my awkward smile, the freckles on my knees, and yes,
even my stretch marks that are merely tiger stripes in his eyes-this he
loves; my imperfections, my flaws, and all that make me uniquely human.

AN INTERESTING QUESTION

Question: Ladies, who is the man of your dreams?

Does he have a Denzel Washington face?

Does he know what's on your mind without you ever saying a word, and knows exactly what to say and do because he's totally in-tune to you?

Is he very romantic and sends you flowers for no reason, never expecting anything in return because it brings him joy just to see you happy?

Is he one who never compares you to his mother or any ex-girlfriends, and always admits when he's wrong because he understands how detrimental this would be to the relationship?

Is he always sensitive to your feelings, very thoughtful and considerate, doesn't have a selfish bone in his body, and never takes you for granted?

Does he love all the weight you've gained and feels that it gives you character?

Is he a firm believer in communication, and a great listener?

Is he one who never does or says anything to make you angry because he thinks before he speaks?

Does he cook for you every day when he gets home from work, and prefers quiet time with you instead of TV or football?

Is he a financial genius, takes care of all the bills while keeping your purse fully loaded with plenty of cash and just absolutely loves it when you spend all his money?

WAKE UP! HE DOESN'T EXIST!

The only perfect man to ever walk the face of this earth was Jesus Christ.

So, who is the man of my dreams, you may ask? He is a God-fearing man, who not only loves me, but appreciates me.

So, fellas…

Question: Who is the woman of your dreams?

Aw, never mind, just go back to sleep and keep dreaming.

MISSING YOU

Sometimes I wonder, do you ever think of me?

Is there always that certain song you would hear on the radio that reminds you of me?

Does the sudden hint of vanilla scented candles make you think about my sweet fragrance that I wear on my skin?

When you think about my smile and how relaxing it was to you, does it put a smile on your face?

Do you ever close your eyes and set your mind in motion, thinking about the last time you saw me, the last time you held me, the last time you kissed me?

Do you wish that you could see me again?

Do you wish that you could be with me?

Are you missing me, like I've been missing you?

THE HOLE

Please, pull me out of this dark hole
I want to see daylight again
If you don't hurry, I'll sink deeper
And your reach will not be within

I've been in this hole way too long
I feel cold, very weak and weary
I'm crying out for some assistance
A voice nearly gone, and eyes that are teary

Your aid in this rescue is urgent
My life, I hope you can save
If no one comes soon to help me
This dark hole will soon be my grave

MELEE IN MY MIND

So many things going on inside my head

The anxiety in my heart grows stronger by the minute, yet I can't put into words what to say

I can't tell you what I want you to know

Fear keeps me quietly suffering inside

Quietly longing, wishing, anticipating something extraordinary, like a sudden burst of free expression of my thoughts and wonders

No longer hiding behind a cloud of confusion

Free to be me, then I can breathe, and exhale a sigh of relief

No more melee in my mind

FEEL SORRY FOR HIM

Her pretty brown eyes are now black and blue.

You see, the love of her life has been pounding his fists into her face and ignored her painful cries, begging him to please don't beat her tonight.   She was too weak to put up a fight because there's no more fight left in her.

But don't feel sorry for her
Feel sorry for him

The next day, the love of her life decided he didn't want her anymore because she was useless in his eyes. He pushed her out the door, and she fell flat on her face, covering the sidewalk in blood and tears.

But don't feel sorry for her
Feel sorry for him

She fears for her life. You see, the one who promised to love and protect her, threatened to kill her because she was still on his property. She wants to run, she wants to hide, but she can't move. Instead she cries out for God to remove her sad plight as she lays there, a broken soul with a crushed spirit.

But don't feel sorry for her
Feel sorry for him

You see, the Bible says we are accountable to God for our actions, and a wicked spirit and wicked works are detestable in His eyes.

The Bible says God is a God of Justice, and will hear and give an answer to the outcries of the long-suffering. "Vengeance belongs to me" says God.

So don't feel sorry for her
Feel sorry for him!

TIME & UNFORSEEN OCCURRENCE

I didn't know this would be the day
That life would change in the blink of an eye
I never told you that I loved you
Or given a chance to say a final good-bye

Had I known the day and hour
Of this very tragic event
I would have taken the opportunity
Of our last moments left to be spent

If I had known that you would suddenly
Take flight like a lone, peaceful dove
I would have expressed my gratitude
And my sincere heartfelt love

Though I miss you so very badly
Circumstances were beyond our control
You lived a full, blessed life
My heart and mind, I must console

Even though I was caught off guard
By the day you would suddenly fall
I take comfort in God's word knowing
Time and unforeseen occurrence befalls us all

UNWORTHY

You stole my heart, and I want it back

Because in your eyes, my heart is just a toy to be played with

You don't know how to care for it, you don't know how to protect it

You fail to recognize what each pulsating heartbeat means as it beats profusely for you

You don't appreciate the warmth and the love that it gives

Your carelessness broke my heart, and now it needs to mend and heal

You stole my heart, and I want it back

Because you don't deserve it

WHAT I FEEL

I feel like a cool breeze
Exhilarating and free
A breeze that's gentle and relaxing
Calming everything around me

I feel like tears that fall from the sky
Tapping against a window pane
Tempting a lazy sleep-in
Enjoying the roof-top sounds of the rain

I feel like I'm at peace with myself
When expressing myself to Jah
At ease and feeling reassured
My faith, ten-times strengthened in awe

SPOIL ME

Spoil me, please, if you would
I wanna know how it feels to be treated good

Massage my back, rub my feet
Hold my hand, call me your sweet

Send me roses, take me on a shopping spree
Buy me nice clothes, shoes, purses, and jewelry

A candlelight dinner, kiss my cheek
Tell me you love me, as you softly speak

Take me for quiet walks out in the park
Watch our favorite movies in the dark

Shower me with chocolates, scented candles, and love
Spoil me if you would please, this is what I dream of

HE SAID

We crossed paths one fall afternoon
Shared some pleasant conversation
Made plans to take a walk under the moon

He said that I was amazing

He said that I was beautiful

He said he loves my smile

He said forever he could hold me, and look deep into my eyes

Is he for real? (Breathe girl)
But I guess time will tell

I'll never forget the love in his voice
The sweet things that he said
Let heaven and earth rejoice!

OUR LIFE IS MUSIC

Celebrating the music we made
And the jazzy cool way that we played

From A-minor to B-flat
Our music is all that

I know sometimes we played off-key
But what we have is like a sweet symphony

Another year is another encore
So happy anniversary, let's keep playing more

We're celebrating the music we made
Our life is music, so glad that we played

WISH I KNEW

Wish I knew if I was on your mind, because I can't read it

If I could swim around deep inside your head, I wonder what would I find?

It kills me when you're so non-chalant

I'm tired of your mixed signals, just tell me what you want

Sometimes I think you dig me, and then sometimes I don't

Always taking me for granted, when you promised me you won't

Maybe I'm just too deep for you

Or for you, it's not that deep

Maybe, I should just let you, and whatever this is, go

Wish I knew if there will ever come a day when you will open up, and maybe, again come my way

Let me know when you feel free, to be who you really want to be

THE ONE THING I CAN'T STAND

I hate foolishness!

It will make you lose your common sense

It will divide and conquer, and leave a hot mess trail of trouble

Just a big pot of chaotic madness that likes to be stirred

The insanity makes you wonder, "Who does this?"

And it can work your nerves (but only if you let it)

See no foolishness
Hear no foolishness
Speak no foolishness
Do no foolishness

And may God bless you!

COLD

I'm shivering in this miserable place
With its icy cold stares and icy cold race

I'm frozen, and I can't seem to get warm
Too many cold shoulders all in a swarm

The temperature is dropping 50 below
A spread sheet of ice before it hits zero

What a horrible place, so frigid, so cold
Out here, you die young before you grow old

PLAYED

Let me tell you the story of a mistake I made
I put my trust in someone, and then I was played

I was made to believe I was the sun, moon and stars
Only to find I was deceived, leaving me with scars

I thought I was desired in his eyes
But it was only an act, to my surprise

He played me like a bass fiddle, sounding deep and strong
So disappointed to learn he had done me wrong

He played me like a saxophone, sounding smooth and cool
I feel so humiliated, I feel like such a fool

I've never in my life felt so used
He wasted my time, my heart he abused

He played with my emotions, and he doesn't care
As if I don't exist, as if I'm not there

I'm still here, but how bad I feel
My pride he's stolen, what more can he steal?

Being played like this, the worst feeling I've ever felt
A situation like this, I've never dealt

I can't trust anyone, it's plain to see
Don't know who's real, or who's lying to me

I've been played once, don't wanna be played again
I may not ever let anyone else in

SISTER GIRL & BROTHER MAN

Sister Girl, why you cryin'?
Sister Girl, are you dyin' from his lyin'?
Don't you know the sun will still shine on you?
So keep your head held high, do away with your blues!

Sister Girl, it ain't worth it
Sister Girl, love yourself
Sister Girl, let go of hurt feelings
Throw 'em out the window, take 'em off the shelf

Brother Man, why you so conniving? Why? Lord Why?
Brother Man, don't even try it, we know you lied, and you lied
Don't you know what's done in the dark will come to the light?
So make your crooked ways straight, and start yourself a new life

Brother Man, was it worth it?
Brother Man, respect yourself
Brother Man, see you all alone now
Forget your foolish pride, don't keep it on the shelf

MIND vs. HEART

As I make a complete U-turn to go back to what's familiar to me and follow my heart, my mind begins to plant seeds of doubt.

Doubting if I ever make it to where I want to be, doubting if my heart can truly lead me to finding true happiness.

I can feel my heart beating faster, stronger, motivating me to pay no mind to my mind , and let my thoughts of doubt disappear.

My heart means well, but it can be treacherous, and it's been known to lead me in the wrong direction.

But I don't want to be lost again.

Which is stronger, the mind or the heart?

My mind begins recalling past experiences of my heart. So many blessed days of my heart being full of love and laughter, but so many other days of my heart being sad and broken.

My mind is making it a point to remind me that what feels right isn't always right.

My heart is saying since it feels right, it must be right.

Which is stronger, the mind or the heart?

I pray for wisdom, I pray for discernment, I pray my choices and decisions will make both my mind and my heart glad, and no longer at war with each other, but working together to achieve my peace of mind and happiness.

OBEY

Feeling uncomfortable in my own home
What once was a haven, is now just a dome

I was told I'm not the way a woman should be
Like the Bible says in Ephesians 5:21-23

I was told it gives o.k. for him to demean me
To humiliate, to mistreat, to rob me of my dignity

If told to bark like a dog, this scripture means do it
If told to jump off a bridge, this scripture means hop to it

But that's how it was explained, and I was so confused
I know these aren't instructions on how to abuse

What about verse 28, "love your wife as your own body?"
But then I was chastised for trying to be a smarty

I was told to never speak up, my role I should not neglect
He said, "I am your head, and you're showing disrespect."

Feeling hopeless and more confused, I begin to wonder
Would I be better off buried six-feet under?

Does God really want me to live this way?
So every night, I close my eyes and pray

Keep my head held high, and just obey
And wait for God to remove the dismay

SOUL FOOD

I know a place that serves all you can eat soul food, 24 hours a day, seven days a week.

Gluttony does not exist here. You can eat as much as you please without the risk of heart disease.

It's free of charge, and the owner warmly invites everyone to partake and get their appetites filled.

So where exactly can this soul food be found? It's in God's word, the Bible. Sample a taste of Galatians 5:22, 23:

Main courses of *Love* and *Joy*, with a slice of *Peace* and *Long-suffering*
Two sides of *Kindness* and *Goodness*
Bread of *Faith* buttered in *Mildness*
And a big old helping of *Self-control*

So be good to your soul and daily feed it.
This is God's soul food, you know you need it!

A FAMILY STRONG

The foundation of a family strong is built on prayer, love and wisdom, a sense of pride, and a large shield of faith to fight the battle of alienation.

For a family strong, survival is unity, not division.

Fathers, mothers, sisters, brothers, together we make a family strong.

MY FEEL GOOD FEELING

Another glorious and beautiful day
My heart overflowing with happiness
My feel good feeling has taken over me
Breaking chains of melancholy that oppress

My feel good feeling brings out the best in me
Glowing like a bright summer's day
I'm in a better frame of mind and could care less
If everything doesn't quite go my way

My feel good feeling mellows me
Taking in life's simple pleasures that abound
I'm so blessed to be able to enjoy these things
I'm so blessed to be alive and still around

My feel good feeling's got me elated
What a wonderful kind of feeling to have
Been so long since I've felt this good
Been so long since I've heard myself laugh

CHILDHOOD

I miss my Barbie dolls, my Easy Bake oven, and my favorite children's book, Charlotte's Web.

I miss making mud pies, riding my little blue bike, and playing with my jump rope.

I miss my little red & yellow book satchel I use to carry to school with my Wonder Woman lunch box.

I miss my paint by number art, my tea sets, my paper dolls, and my pink hula hoop.

I miss the big yarn ribbons I wore in my hair, and those little corduroy bell bottoms I sported with the matching flower and paisley vest.

I miss that little girl that I use to be. I miss my childhood.

Back then, little girls just enjoyed being little girls.

They didn't experience the pressures to grow up fast and to be shaped and molded into scandalous party queens, and drop it like it's hot video vixens.

Little girls, love who you are, and enjoy your childhood.

IN DENIAL (I THINK HE LOVES ME)

We never go out together
No dinner and a movie, no long walks in the park
No sweet, sentimental conversations
Forbidden in the daylight, but welcomed after dark

He never says "I love you", like I'd want him to
So I can say " I love you too"
So I won't say it, because he won't say it
But the way he holds me says he do
And the way he kissed me says he do

Yeah, I think he loves me
He's always running back into my arms, so what else could it be?

He will always give me nothing
No chocolates, pearls or diamonds, no just because bouquet
No cards, e-mails, or text messages
Just to say I'm on his mind and how was your day

He never says "I need you", like I'd want him to
So I can say "I need you too"
So I won't say it, because he won't say it
But the way he holds me says he do
And the way he kissed me says he do

Yeah, I think he loves me
He's always running back into my arms, so what else could it be?

NEGATIVITY

I gotta push it away, far away from me
All this negativity

Always bringin' me down, way down
Too much of it going around
It shatters my pride, and will humiliate
It kills my spirit, tortures my soul, and makes me hate

I just can't deal with it today
Negativity, please, just go away

I gotta run far away, I gotta go and hide
From your ugly, negative vibe

It might rub off on me and spread
And like terminal cancer I'll be dead

Can't enjoy life, eat, sleep, laugh or love
Negativity so strong, can't give praise above

I gotta kick it to the curb before it catches me
All that negativity

Be gone with ya' bad self, and oh yeah, guess what?
Try to come back again, I'll kick your butt!

I just can't deal with it today
Negativity, please, just go away

I will win the challenge, I will win the fight
Negativity, negativity, it just ain't right

TAKE ME AWAY

Take me away, far away from here
Help me release my fear, please hold me near
Take me away

You said that we could go and get away
From all the pressure and the strain
All I have to do is say the word
Whether it's bus or plane

Take me away, I need serenity
I need some peace you see, please comfort me
Take me away

You said that we could leave tonight at eight
And travel with the moon and stars
All I have to do is pack my bags
Together we'll go far

Take me away
Far away from here
Please, let's get away
In your arms I'll stay

THE WICKED ONE

This world is so full of animosity and hate
It can quickly lock you into its treacherous gate

Acts of violence bubbling forth like water in fountains
Senseless deaths stacking up as tall as mountains

Pain, persecution, nation against nation
Hungry for peace, but suffering from starvation

The wicked one is in full command
The wicked one plays a deadly hand

A deadly hand in the violence we see
The crimes, the terrorism, and the misery

Leaving us afraid, scared, and dumbfounded
But we pray, and we pray, to keep ourselves grounded

Like the sands of an hour glass
So this too shall pass

So falls the last grain of sand
Against God and His kingdom
The wicked one will no longer stand

RANDOM THOUGHTS

My random thoughts...

When expectations shatter like broken glass, pick up the pieces carefully.

How can I take you there if you won't tell me where to go?

Since God is good all the time, and all the time God is good, why do so many keep disrespecting Him and His creation?

Sometimes, people just don't get me, but that's alright.

If I only had a time machine (enough said).

It must be painful to love others, because the world is full of so much hate.

Is simple complexity simply complex?

Would falling asleep be an insomniac's dream?

Why do people always miss my point and go left field?

We sail on the same seas of life, in the same boat, and we still can't get along.

How come no one will teach me how to Dougie?

I wonder how many grandchildren will I have?

If my soulmate is out there, where you at? Come on man!

More money, more problems. No money, more problems. Same drama, same difference.

But when will that million dollar check be dropped in my mailbox?

I guess if I had a dime for every time somebody treated me shady, I'd have my millions and my sons would never want for nothing.

Sometimes, when you've done the best that you could, the results aren't always successful.

Will the electric slide ever die?

What would it be like to live forever?

I love my family.

If I had Halle Berry's radiance, Lena Horne's grace, a Beyonce strut, and some Tina Turner legs, would you think I was tha' bomb?

And why didn't Annie Mae eat the cake?

 My random thoughts…

MY #1 FAN

I am a superstar.

I'm Hollywood, I'm big time, rollin' like a boss, and I didn't even know it, until your messy relentless ways made it all clear to me.

You are my #1 fan.

I consume your thoughts 24/7. You can't get me off your mind.

You can't stop talking about me. Your entire conversation revolves around me and what I do.

Your every move depends on "my" every move, because you can't plot and plan unless you know what I'm doing.

You can't eat, sleep or breathe without me. I live in your dreams, and I am the reason you wake up every morning.

Your whole life revolves around me, and only me. It's all about me.

So let me give a shout out to you, my #1 fan:

Get a life!

THANK YOU

T hank you *Jehovah* for not only giving me the love of art and writing, but also the courage to do what I've always wanted to do, to publish my first book of poetry, and to not be afraid of criticism or what others may think or say.

To all of my family, friends, and some of the most talented and amazing poets, writers, and spoken word artists I've had the pleasure of meeting, I sincerely thank you for your love and support, and your encouragement to "keep writing". And a special thank you to my biggest supporter, my sister, Christy Goines-Large, owner of Kreashuns Graphics Group, who worked diligently on the design and layout of this publication.

And thank you for reading Expressions Inspired!

THE
INSPIRATION

Was there something you read that touched your heart, aroused your curiosity or maybe made you wonder "just what was she thinking?" I've included a little something extra, the inspiration behind the poetry. Whether it was something personal, a random thought, a song on the radio, or whatever I saw or heard, if it moved me, I wrote about it. Enjoy!

My Rights (2005)-My way of giving myself an attitude adjustment.

What I Got (2013)-Enduring this economy as a single parent, and my insomnia.

Words (2013)-For conniving, relentless people who, apparently, their only mission in life is to tear other people down.

"I" (2004)-I received a card one day from one of the sisters who was in my congregation at the time. The card encouraged me to stay encouraged and keep enduring.

Go Deep (2004)-I thought about how easy it would be to understand others if we could go inside their minds and know how they feel or what they're thinking.

We Do Need You (2004)-Listening to a song by Jill Scott called "The Fact Is". It's a song about women who can do for themselves, but humbly acknowledges the fact that as women, we do need our men in our lives.

Who We Be (2005)-Listening to the radio to one of my favorites from the 90's, Arrested Development's version of "Everyday People."

The Truth (2012)-I thought about the dictionary meaning of the truth, and wondered if the truth was an actual strong, confident, woman, how would she describe herself? And this is what I came up with.

You Don't Cry No More (2004)-For my parents helping me get through some rough times.

Sisters (2004)-For my own sister, my best friends, my spiritual sisters, my relatives, and other friends and acquaintances I admire. Much love and appreciation for you!

The New Me Realization (2012)-After looking at myself in the mirror one day, and realizing just how much I have physically changed in the past 10 or 15 years or so. Skinny left me a long time ago!

Who Do You Think You Are? (2012)-Laughing and talking with one of my friends about the "love at first sight" theory. I'm still laughing about that one!

Falling (2012)-In what unique way of words would I let someone know I was interested in him and would like to know him better? I came up with this snippet.

Speechless (2004)-I thought about this young girl I use to work with a few years ago who always talked about her long hugs goodbye with her boyfriend. I remember that feeling.

That Kiss (2003)-Reminiscing, and that's all I have to say about that!

You Can't Hide (2004)-Aggravated with someone who lied to me and refused to tell the truth.

Learn Who I Am (2013)-So many people who suffer from depression. It shouldn't be overlooked or taken lightly.

Soulful Respect (2004)-A conversation with a friend about using Jesus as a role model to follow when you're in a relationship.

It's Not You (2012)-A conversation I had with a co-worker one day about how some women, both younger and older, allow certain degrading, disrespectful treatment from their mates or boyfriends just for the sake of saying "I got a man" or "I'm in a relationship". It is so not worth your dignity!

Who Can Stand? (2005)-Of course, this is only about Satan the Devil.

The System (2004)- I was upset one day about people who are in a position to help guide our children in the right direction, but behave just like children themselves. Children imitate what they see.

Wide Open (2005)-After reading a collection of 19th century African-American poetry about bondage and discrimination, I thought, if I was a slave, how would I describe the feeling of being set free?

Tranquility (2004)-I was soaking in the tub one evening after a long day at work, and I could hear my sons, who were ages 8 and 5 at the time, playing and laughing in the next room.

Initiative (2005)- Thinking about how so many people were coming to the aid of others who were suffering from hurricanes and other natural disasters.

Chocolate Child (2005)-Although this can apply to any teenage girl, I thought about the young, black teenage girl who "thinks" she knows it all. We all know one or two of them, or maybe that was once you.

Love Hopeless (2006)-One of my favorite songs came on the radio, "Hopeless" by Dionne Farris, and although her song wasn't specifically about love, I started thinking about what would having a "hopeless" love for someone be like.

Under The Scope (2004)-One of those days when it seemed like everyone around me was literally on my back and questioning my actions. This is not a good feeling at all.

Misunderstood (2012)-So many past and present situations where someone just totally got the wrong understanding about me, and perceives me in a negative light.

Colors (2004)-A partial rainbow I saw got me thinking, if you had to describe yourself through colors, which color would you be and how would you do it? Deciding not to limit myself to just one color, this is what I came up with.

You & I (2012)-I read a pamphlet about the different types of domestic abuse and how to recognize the signs. Domestic abuse is not limited to a physical action of mistreatment, but also verbal and emotional mistreatment as well.

Set Yourself Free (2004)-I wrote this after having a long talk with one of my friends who was having a tough time with a life-changing event. I felt so bad for her, but also, I could relate to what she was feeling at the time.

What He Loves (2012)-Just my thoughts on how nice it would be to find someone who loved you just for being you.

An Interesting Question (2012)-I remember about 5 or 6 years ago, an old friend of mine asked what do I want in a husband if I ever decided to re-marry. Some, but not all, of the things I thought I wanted at that time was totally unrealistic. I had a good laugh thinking about that and how much my view has changed since then. No one, including ourselves, is perfect. If you're seeking perfection in someone, you will never find it!

Missing You (2012)-After hearing Tamia's "Officially Missing You" on the radio, one of my favorites.

The Hole (2004)- For the life of me, I can't remember what exactly happened to move me to write this one. My notes that I scribbled only said "a dark moment". Something must have upset me pretty bad at that time, so I took it out on my pen and paper.

Melee In My Mind (2006)-One day, I asked my oldest son, who was 10 years old at the time, how was school. He said that all of his thoughts keep fighting each other, so he didn't know what to tell me about first. He always had an interesting way of putting things.

Feel Sorry For Him (2004)-My thoughts on domestic abuse. Behind closed doors, it may not be readily noticed by others, but God sees all.

Time and Unforeseen Occurrence (2004)-Ecclesiastes 9:11. A co-worker died a sudden death that year, and as far as anyone knew, she had no health issues of any sort.

Unworthy (2013)-A discussion I had with one of my friends about guarding your heart because not everyone is worthy of it.

What I Feel (2004)-This was about one of the most peaceful days I've ever had, and it felt good!

Spoil Me (2004)-Hey, what can I say, it's what I want. It may seem a little superficial, but deep down inside I think all women would like those things sometime, if not all the time.

He Said (2004)-I received a compliment from someone who said I was amazing, so I just played off of that, and came up with this.

Our Life is Music (2004)-I wanted to write about married couples who have celebrated their lives together as husband and wife. To be married 20 plus years is both a milestone and a blessing.

Wish I Knew (2004)-"Talk To Me" by Anita Baker, she's asking what's wrong with you and why don't you tell me what you're going through. There's always that one person in that one relationship that you just can't quite figure out because they won't be completely open with you.

The One Thing I Can't Stand (2012)-No surprise here. Like everyone else, I really can't stand foolishness and the unnecessary drama that comes with it.

Cold (2004)-Being in a place around people who made me feel unwelcome; just a cold and unfriendly atmosphere.

Played (2004)-I had a conversation one day with some coworkers, and we were laughing and comparing stories about the so-called "players" and heartbreakers back in high school.

Sister Girl & Brother Man (2004)- I was being checked out at a grocery store, and my cashier was telling the cashier in the other lane about her bad breakup with her boyfriend. She sounded as if her life was over.

Mind vs. Heart (2012)-Jeremiah 17:9. A bible discussion about how treacherous the heart can be and how, sometimes, it can cause you to make bad choices.

Obey (2004)-One of my friends told me that her husband read Ephesians 5:21-23 to her and literally said to her that this scripture means if he tells her to bark like a dog, she has to do it. I never forgot that, and I always wonder how many more husbands out there take this scripture to that extreme. This couple is no longer together, by the way.

Soul Food (2004)-Galatians 5:22, 23 What we need, the fruitages of the spirit: love, joy, peace, long-suffering, kindness, goodness, faith, mildness, and self-control.

A Family Strong (2004)-Love and appreciation for the Robinson and Goines family, my family!

My Feel Good Feeling (2004)-Simply feeling good about myself.

Childhood (2013)-Thinking back when I was a little girl and how simple life was. Today, our girls don't have many decent role models to follow.

In Denial (I Think He Loves Me) (2011)-I was in a department store dressing room, trying on some sundresses. In the dressing rooms beside me, I could hear an older lady talking to a younger lady about the current "relationship" she was in. Apparently, the young lady was crazy in love with this guy, but he did not feel this way about her. The older lady said to her, "You're being forbidden in the daylight, but welcomed after dark. It's gonna get old. Don't you think you deserve better than that?" That stuck in my mind for the rest of the day. It had been a while since I had written anything, but I suddenly felt moved to write about that.

Negativity (2004)-At one point I was hearing so much gossip and slander and back-biting talk, and watching others humiliate people and throw them under the bus, it got to be too over-whelming.

Take Me Away (2004)-This was based on a dream I had one night. It was pretty cool.

The Wicked One (2013)-The growing increase of violence and crime, and it's all Satan's work.

Random Thoughts (2013)-Anytime I had a random thought, no matter how serious or how silly it was, I wrote it down. They're only thoughts.

My #1 Fan (2013)-This is for anyone that's ever had someone whose whole life seems to center around destroying you and your character.

www.ingramcontent.com/pod-product-compliance
Lightning Source LLC
Chambersburg PA
CBHW062027040426
42447CB00010B/2167